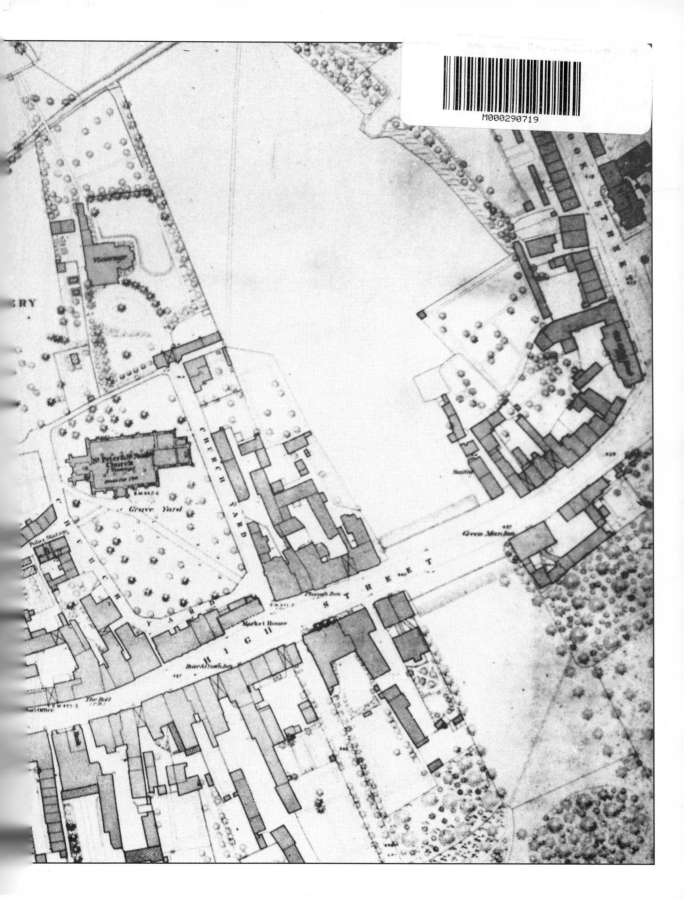

TRING

A Pictorial History

The post office *c*.1900 with the horse and carriage from Pendley being driven by Mr. Williams whose family rebuilt Pendley Manor in 1835 after the fire.

TRING

A Pictorial History

Barry Woodhouse

Phillimore

1996

Published by
PHILLIMORE & CO. LTD.
Shopwyke Manor Barn, Chichester, West Sussex

ISBN 1 86077 017 7

Printed and bound in Great Britain by
BIDDLES LTD.
Guildford, Surrey

To my parents, brother, relations and old school friends. To Tring, Surrey Place, and Akeman Street. For those early years and many happy memories,
Thank you.

List of Illustrations

Frontispiece: High Street scene

Acknowledgements

Public Records Office, Kew; Public Reference Library, Aylesbury; Central Counties Newspapers, The Bucks Herald Archives, Aylesbury; Reverend J.A.S. Payne Cook, M.A., St Peter and St Paul Parish Church, Tring; The Luton Museum, Wardown Park, Luton; June Lawson, Barton Hills, Luton.

Illustration Acknowledgements

Most of the photographs in this book are from the author's own collection. He would like to thank the organisations and individual people who have kindly permitted him to use their photographs, prints and maps in this book. Particular thanks are due to Anna Eavis of the National Monuments Records Office for her help in tracing copyright holders of some of the illustrations used.

Royal Commission on the Historical Monuments of England, Swindon, 13-14, 24, 35, 38-9, 42, 44-5, 95, 132-3 © RCHME Crown Copyright; Hertford Museum, Hertford, 17, 20, 55, 101, front and back end papers; The National Portrait Gallery, London, 19, 20, by courtesy of the National Portrait Gallery; B.T. Batsford Ltd., London, 6; Mr. Keith Skone, Keytone Publications, Sutton, 100, 119; Mr. Robert Grace, Tring, frontispiece, 2, 5, 7, 9, 21-3, 31, 50-1, 62-3, 67-70, 80, 82, 86, 88, 91, 103, 97, 104-7, 109-10, 111-15, 122-23, 125-27, 137, 140-42, 144, 148-49, 156, 162, 170-71; Mr. Mike Bass, Tring, 1, 48, 53, 57, 59, 73-4, 79, 87, 94, 98, 102-3, 120-21, 131, 139, 147, 150-51, 155, 168, 172-5; Mr. and Mrs. Gena Neale, Tring, 36.

Photographs of Tring in the 1990s were taken by the author, while other photographs before this period have been purchased over the years and form part of an extensive collection.

Introduction

Tring is situated in a small valley within the Chiltern Hills on the southern border of Buckinghamshire. A market town since 1315, the town was born at the crossing of two very old Roman routes—the Icknield Way and Akeman Street.

Early settlers to the area were probably attracted by the ample supply of water from the chalk hills of the Chilterns which Tring nestles amongst. Beneath these hills a lowland clearing followed water courses to what is now known as New Mill, and would have been ideal for early man.

The area has been inhabited since about 2000 B.C. The remains of a Beaker burial dating from this time was discovered along the line of the old Roman Akeman Street and was reported in the *Victoria County History of Hertfordshire* printed in 1905. (The custom of the 'Beaker' folk was to bury with the body clay beakers of some four pints' capacity.) British coins from 15 B.C.-A.D. 40 which were discovered at nearby Bulbourne provide yet further evidence of early settlements, while at Wigginton, just outside Tring, Bronze- and Iron-age finds were made in 1858 during ploughing on the common and included a bronze knife with a bone handle carved into the shape of a dog's head. At nearby Aldbury a hoard of British and Roman coins was discovered by workers building a new road at the Bridgewater Monument in Ashridge during 1870. Roman pottery has also been discovered at Bulbourne and Tringford. In the British Museum is a Roman legionnaire's helmet which was unearthed during the digging of the Grand Junction (now Grand Union) canal outside Tring in 1813.

The name Tring has changed many times over the centuries. The town has been known as 'Tredunga', 'Tredunge', 'Treung', 'Treunge', 'Trenge', 'Treng' and 'Trynge'; these are but a few of the many variations to the name Tring as we know it today. At some time after the 15th century the 'e' appears to have been changed to an 'i'. Domesday Book also records many variations to the spelling of Tring. Icknield was once known as 'Ecknell' which changed to 'Icknell' (again the 'e' changes to 'i') and later became Icknield. There is an Upper Icknield Way and a Lower Icknield Way. Both these branches begin in Ivinghoe just outside Tring, where the top road, Upper Icknield Way, runs through to Wendover and the bottom road, Lower Icknield Way, runs to Buckland. The Icknield Way, although of Roman origin, was a road of the old Iceni kingdom, and the name Icknield is derived from the Iceni name of ancient Britons. Akeman Street was a major Roman road running from St Albans in the south east to Cirencester in the west.

The actual meaning of the name Tring has been lost in the past but it has been suggested by some historians that it is derived from 'third', being a third of a hundred, as in the Chiltern Hundreds, or that it could mean 'a place of trees' from the Saxon name 'Tre'. Many Saxon names end with 'ing', meaning 'something that belongs'. Hence 'Treing—trees that belong', or 'a place of trees'. There is an old rhyme which says:

Bulbourne was a city
When St Albans was a wood
Tring was a little place
And never any good.

There are several reported instances of ghostly apparitions which include a Roman soldier in full battle order being seen at Miswell, a skirmish between Queen Boudicca and Roman soldiers along Duncombe Terrace, and an 'army' of Romans on Wigginton Common. This was reported in the *Bucks Advertiser* of July 1835 and was seen for several mornings at 6 o'clock.

The manor of Tring was held by a priest named Engelric prior to the Norman Conquest. William the Conqueror's land policy meant that Norman over-lords were brought into the manor and Tring passed to Eustace II of Boulogne. Eustace II's granddaughter inherited the manor from Eustace III. She married Henry I's nephew (1125) Stephen of Blois (a grandson of William the Conqueror). Stephen founded St Saviour's at Faversham in Kent and the grant of the Manor of Tring (*Manerium de Treangre*) was confirmed in 1175 by Henry II. The abbots of Faversham each in succession became lord of the manor which in 1278 was said to be worth £30 a year. The grant of a market made on 23 July 1315 by Edward II permitted a market each Tuesday and a fair for 10 days each year. The manor was let (1316) for £90 a year to John de Pelham, the king's clerk marshal. The Black Death afflicted Tring during 1349 when 'a number of people died'. The Peasants Revolt of May to July 1381 was caused mainly by a severe economic depression because of the Hundred Years War with France and increased taxation in 1377, 1379 and yet again in 1381. The fear of a French invasion together with resentment over these tax increases finally forced the revolt. A Richard Horsman from the Kings Langley area led a band of rebels in Tring during June, when books, title deeds and other records of the manor belonging to the Archbishop of Canterbury were destroyed. Rebels from Tring also took part in a demonstration at St Albans on Sunday 16 June.

The Hertfordshire rebels were unlike others, they were not plunderers nor political opportunists, but desired only to have certain rights, such as to be able to pasture their cattle, to fish and to grow and mill their own corn. On 13 December 1381 the King, at the request of Parliament, granted an amnesty by a general act. Only four rebels from Hertfordshire were not granted remission, none of whom came from Tring.

In 1546 the manor of Tring was in the king's gift (Henry VIII) to Sir Edward North, who conveyed the manor to Sir Richard Lee. Queen Mary Tudor granted the manor in 1555 to Henry Peckham for services to the crown, but Henry Peckham was convicted of plotting against the crown (the Tudor conspiracy) and was executed on 7 July 1556. On the death of Elizabeth (Henry Peckham's widow) the manor went to the crown until 1679 when Henry Guy became lord of the manor. Henry Guy was a confidant of Charles II. Guy's home was in Tring Park, and was designed and built by Sir Christopher Wren. Henry Guy sold it to Sir William Gore some time before 1700 and William Gore's son, Charles, had the manor from 1739-68 when it was sold to Sir Drummond Smith who died 'without issue'. The estate was disposed of in 1823 by trustees to William Kay. During his ownership it was rented to various people including Nathan Mayer Rothschild as a summer residence, until it was purchased at auction in 1872 by Lionel Nathan de Rothschild together with Tring Park, altogether approximately

3,643 acres, for £230,000. Included in the sale were a brew house, venison house, the *Green Man Inn*, a silk mill and various shops and houses. Lionel's son, Nathaniel (Natty), came to Tring in 1874 and became Lord Rothschild of Tring in 1885. When he died in 1915 he was described as 'the richest man in the British Empire'.

The mansion has a very colourful history. There were many royal visitors to the house and one story is that Charles II (1630-85) used to visit with a certain Nell Gwyn (Eleanor Gwyn 1650-87), an orange seller and comic actress from the streets of Drury Lane, who became the mistress of Lord Buckhurst and also of the king himself.

In the woods in the park is an obelisk supposedly built to commemorate Nell Gwyn's visits to the mansion with King Charles II. There has been considerable research into this story, but it has never been proved or disproved. Nathaniel Rothschild undertook some investigations into the story, but he could find no evidence to substantiate the legend, although it was thought that Charles II gave the house and grounds to Nell Gwyn.

The Rothschild banking family had a major influence on Tring and its people when they moved there in 1872 and settled in the mansion in Tring Park. The coming of Nathaniel Rothschild and his wife Emma brought for the town and its population many changes which would dramatically change their lives and that of Tring for ever. Some time after their arrival Nathaniel cleared away slum houses at the rear of Akeman Street and built 50 modern cottages which he presented to the town council. One condition was that for the first year the tenants would only be charged 'a nominal rent'. As well as these cottages he also undertook to rebuild several hundred cottages on the Tring Park Estate.

Other improvements which Nathaniel and Emma undertook included more slum clearances, supporting local industries, building an Isolation Hospital (following an outbreak of typhoid), founding the Chiltern Hills Spring Water Company, the organisation of a health service for Tring (for a yearly subscription of £1 anyone qualified for free medical attention), and free nursing. Emma Rothschild built and equipped a nursing home. All employees on the Tring Park Estate enjoyed these services free of charge. At the time there was no national health service nor indeed any other type of health service.

The Louisa Alms Cottages in Park Road were built by Emma in memory of her mother Louisa for the use of retired employees of the Tring Park Estate. Allotments were made available for everybody in Tring which could be leased from the Estate offices for a small sum. Any man from Tring who wanted a job would be found work in the park woods, and working for the Park Estates was regarded by many as 'insurance from the cradle to the grave'.

Nathaniel died on 31 March 1915 aged 75. His wife Emma died at Home Farm (now called White Cloud Farm) aged 91 on 7 January 1935.

Nathaniel's son Walter was born in 1868. He was to become famous throughout the world for his remarkable knowledge of natural history. It was Walter who collected and displayed the exhibits in what is now The Walter Rothschild Zoological Museum in Akeman Street. The museum opened to the public in 1892, when Walter was 24 years old, attracting 30,000 visitors a year. As there was no public transport and very few cars this is a remarkable figure, particularly as the museum was never advertised nor even signposted!

Anyone who visits his museum in Tring is always astounded by the exhibits: the collections from all parts of the world of animals, birds, butterflies, moths and fish, many of which were prepared by Walter, including the gorilla in the ground-floor display case in which he took great pride. His mother Emma built Tring Museum on the site of Tring Town Farm as a 21st birthday present for him. It was designed by a local architect, William Huckvale, and was built by Tring builders, J. Honour and Sons for the sum of £3,300 which included a cottage for Walter. Walter's first museum was in Albert Street in c.1878 and consisted of a shed at the bottom of the garden. In 1908 new wings of the museum were added for him by Emma and his brother Charles. It now assumed its final form with floor space of some one and a half acres. In the park roamed animals such as zebra, kangaroo, wild horses, emus, rhea, wild turkeys, a tame wolf, several species of deer, cranes, a maraboo stork, a flock of kiwis and giant tortoises. It must have been quite a sight to see deer and other animals not native to this country roaming free, although fallow deer had been there since the days of Sir William Gore.

Walter died in his sleep of cancer on the morning of 27 August 1937 at Home Farm (White Cloud Farm) in Park Road. With his death an era came to an end. He gave the museum together with its exhibits and collections to the Trustees of the British Museum (Walter had been a member of the Trustees from 1899) on condition that the museum became an annex of the Natural History Museum and that it remained a centre for research—which it has done to this day.

A strange story about Walter occurred a few years after his death. It concerns the curator of the flea collection, F.G.A.M. Smit, who reported a very strange event when he was working late at the museum. He heard the sound of very heavy footsteps along the floorboards. As they sounded familiar he did not take a great deal of notice, until he suddenly realised that what he had heard were the footsteps of Walter Rothschild! Not only that, but another employee, Phyllis Thomas, had also heard these same footsteps on a previous occasion. Over the next few years he heard the footsteps between 8 and 11 o'clock in the evenings together with the sound of drawers being opened and closed.

The museum which Walter loved so much is open throughout the year except for the Christmas period. It is located at the junction of Akeman Street and Park Street.

———————

It is thought that Tring has probably had a church since the time of Emperor Constantine in A.D. 337. This belief is based on a Roman coin which was found on the line of old Akeman Street and dated from the time of Emperor Constantine, when Christianity was recognised throughout the Roman Empire. When the wooden structure was replaced by stone during the Norman period is uncertain, but if you look closely enough there are traces of Norman gargoyles which were built back into the restored exterior of the present church. The parish church is dedicated to St Peter and St Paul and incumbents' names date back to the early 1200s. The chantry was added in the early 1300s and at about the same time the chancel floor was relaid. There have been many changes to the structure of the church over the centuries. In the 1400s restoration work was undertaken and major renovations took place in the 19th century after a survey of the church in 1816 revealed that the roof and upper structure were in need of urgent repair work. No more burials were allowed inside the church and restoration work commenced in 1861; two more bells were added in 1882 before the church re-opened in March of the same year; the clock also dates from this period. A guild of brotherhood thrived between 1300 and 1547, and the vestry records show the payments from parish rates up to 1868. A monument to Sir William Gore, who held the manor of Tring and lived in the mansion before 1700 is in the church. He was a Lord Mayor of London as well as a founder member of the Bank of England.

The Rectory House was used in 1718 as a 'house of maintenance' for the use of parishioners. They were given jobs: pillow lace and straw plaiting for the women and outside tasks for the men. Church records show the house master was paid £25 a year in 1740 rising to £525 in 1775. Bread and bacon doles were common during the middle 1790s because of hardship among the labouring classes. By 1815 the cost of the workhouse was exceeding £2,000 per year.

George Washington, the first President of the United States of America, had family connections with Tring. The church register of baptisms has entries for the children of a Reverend Lawrence Washington: Lawrence (1635), Elizabeth (1636) and William (1641). Lawrence (the son) left Tring for Virginia where he purchased land in 1659. He returned to Tring in 1660 and gave up his house and land in Tring before marrying a Maria Jones from Luton. Lawrence returned to Virginia to settle there in 1676. There is also an entry in the church records for the burial of Mrs. Amphyllis Washington, their mother, on 19 June 1654. Letters of administration were given to her son John who was the President's great-grandfather.

Industry in Tring was mainly pillow lace making and straw plaiting for the hat trade. The silk mill in Brook Street employed approximately 600 people in the 1830s; the top wage for a skilled man was about 75 pence per week, with children earning 15 pence. In Akeman Street and Frogmore Street there were lace schools that took children from five years of age to learn the trade as well as teaching them the alphabet (the parents were charged one penny a week for this). As the lace making industry declined, due largely to French imports and mechanisation, straw plaiting grew. This was a cottage industry and payments were calculated at so much per length of plait. Lengths were 10, 20, or 40 yards. The measures would be found by marks cut into the wooden mantelpieces of the cottages. Before the straw could be used it had to be bundled up and bleached; the rougher plait was made from whole straws and the finer from split straw which was passed through a cutter. As lace making was affected by imports, so too was straw plaiting, and the trade gradually died out due to the import of plait mainly from the Far East as well as Italy. An exhibition on straw plaiting is in the Arts and Craft section of the Mossman Museum in nearby Luton.

Silk weaving was another industry at the time, and a silk weaving shop was run by a Mr. Evans at number 60 Akeman Street. Mr. Cato had a canvas weaving shop in Langdon Street which later moved to Charles Street until it closed in the 1920s.

The Victoria Hall is situated at the High Street end of Akeman Street and was erected in 1886 on the site of the former assembly rooms, which were built in 1825. The name was changed to Victoria Works when it produced mineral water, cider, pickled onions and vinegar. It later resumed its former name of Victoria Hall and housed Tring Library for many years. The building was designed by William Huckvale.

Altogether there were at least seventeen public houses in Tring during the 1800s, which is quite a large number to cater for the drinking needs of a total population of under 4,500 including women and children.

The *Bell* in the High Street is one of the oldest surviving in Tring. Records of 1611 show that the landlord, a Henry Geary, was summoned before the justices for keeping the *Bell* without a licence and a few years later he was again in front of them for drunkenness. The building has been heavily restored over the years; the archway was a former right of way, and over it was hung meat and game, which was later cooked at the inn.

The *Britannia* at the end of Western Road and the *King's Arms* on the junction of King Street and Park Road were both built in the early 1830s for the navvies working on the London to Birmingham railway by John Brown of the Tring Brewery Company. The Tring Brewery yard and buildings are still in existence in the High Street, although they are no longer used for brewing. The archway into the old yard still has the name over the top of it.

The *Castle* was built in the early 1840s (probably 1842) and is reputed to be haunted. Built by bargees, it has stables for horses to the rear. It is located opposite the Downs in Park Road on the corner of Langdon Street.

The *Green Man* was part of Tring manor. It was in the lower High Street near the wall at the bottom of Nell Gwyn's Avenue. One of the grooms from the estate would take down to the *Green Man* a tame wolf which was Walter Rothschild's. Once there he would provoke a fight between the wolf (the locals were not aware that it was a wolf) and one of their dogs for a wager! The groom was finally found out and was sacked by Walter who could not abide any cruelty to animals.

Another very old inn situated on the corner of Brook Street is the *Robin Hood* dating from the 17th century. Much of the building has been restored and altered. It was held by a William Tapping in 1806. During 1928 it was owned by the Ivinghoe Brewery of Roberts and Wilson.

Without a doubt the best known inn is the *Rose and Crown*. The original *Rose and Crown* was mentioned in 1620 when it was in the hands of Thomas Robinson. Excise offices were at the inn from the middle of the 17th to the middle of the 19th centuries and beer was brewed there up to the early 1860s. The London and North Western Railway Company had its booking office there, and later the Inland Revenue also had an office. The original inn came level with the pavement and had three stories with dormer windows, tiled roof and an archway entrance to the yard at the rear which had large grounds, large enough for a bowling green. Fairs and circuses were also held there. It was purchased by the Rothschild family who demolished the old building and rebuilt new premises in 1905 mainly to accommodate guests from the mansion when there were no rooms available for them. The new *Rose and Crown* was designed by William Huckvale.

The *Royal Oak* was used for tax appeals and law and order and is now the site of Rodwell's soft drinks offices in Akeman Street. Bank Alley which runs alongside the site of the inn was at one time called Oak Alley.

Dating back to the late 1700s the *Swan* is now a private house at the top of Akeman Street. In 1799 it was described as 'a house and garden'. It was also one of the last farm breweries to function.

It is generally thought that Tring Show saw its beginning in the *Harcourt Arms* (now the *Royal Hotel*) at the railway station in 1839. Mainly a flower and garden produce show, it moved to Tring Park in 1875, expanding to become a fully-fledged agricultural show attracting some 20,000 visitors. At the end of the show visitors would be treated to a firework display. Walter Rothschild was a promoter of the early sheep dog trials and also awarded the prizes. The shows stopped before the Second World War but continued after the war finished up to *c.*1950.

Tring knew how to celebrate special events. When news of the victory at the Battle of Waterloo was received (22 June 1815) the bells rang out all day. Two houses in Akeman Street caught fire when sparks from the bonfire burning an effigy of

Napoleon Bonaparte set light to the thatched roofs. At the end of the Crimean War (29 May 1856) all the shops were closed for the day and there were bonfires during the night; no cottages were reported on fire! The Golden Jubilee of Queen Victoria (21 June 1887) was well reported in *The Bucks Herald*; there was a procession through the High Street, and a march past by Tring volunteers starting from the National School to the Green Man Meadow. For the Diamond Jubilee (22/23 June 1897) some 1,500 children were presented with a medal and given tea. The older generation received a grocery ticket worth 2s. 6d. Also in 1897 the Prince of Wales was a guest of the Rothschilds at the mansion; on this occasion the street was decorated with bunting and flags to celebrate the visit and the gates to the mansion were illuminated with electric lights. Another bonfire celebration took place for the coronation of Edward VII (26 June 1902). The mansion gates were again illuminated by electric lights for the occasion.

Yet there were times when the feelings of Tring people were very mixed. At the end of the First World War (11 November 1918) there was joy because the 'war to end all wars' was finally over, and sadness because of those who would not return home to Tring. The town was very quiet mourning the fallen.

The first school in Tring was founded in 1692 for boys only, the benefactor being Sarah, Duchess of Somerset. A number of educational establishments followed after this time, but as they were not required to conform to a code of practice nor to keep any accounts there is consequently a lack of documentation of their existence or what they achieved. In 1838 there was a school in the Manor House which was later destroyed by fire *c.*1842.

The Tring National School existed from *c.*1842 and was located at the top of the High Street for approximately 100 boys and 70 girls in different buildings. In 1860-70 the school expanded due to the increase in the number of children who were now able to attend. During the First World War the school was used as a military hospital and the children were moved to the Lecture Hall (boys) and the Western Hall (girls) until the war ended. 1931 saw the boys and girls combining when the old girls' school became the Junior Mixed and the boys' side was the Senior Mixed. Mortimer Hill became an extension of these schools in 1947-48 with the construction of a number of single-storey temporary buildings. It was not until 1957 that a brand new school was built next to these buildings. The old school and school house in the High Street closed shortly after 1957 and remained derelict for a number of years until they were demolished in the 1980s.

The Grand Junction Canal was opened in 1805 and Tring summit is the highest navigable waterway in England with a fall of 400 feet along two-and-a-quarter miles, and a total of 57 locks. The reservoirs of Startops, Marsworth, Tringford and Wilstone were constructed to supply water to the canal system, the levels being controlled by the pumping station at Little Tring. The canal from Little Tring was drained mainly because it became unnavigable after the constant loss of water from leaks. It is now dry to Buckland Wharf with only a shallow depth of water from there to Wendover. There are plans now to re-open this stretch and make the canal navigable again from Little Tring to Wendover. Tring wharf in New Mill, which had a windmill until 1911, also made boats, and all manner of goods were brought along the canal system from Birmingham and London. Flour, grain and malt was taken from the mill, and coal, bricks and other building materials were brought in by barge. The flour mill next to the canal bridge now stands where the windmill stood.

It was not until 1837 that the railway arrived at Tring to compete with the canals and the roads for passengers and freight. Tring Town railway station is actually some two miles outside the town towards the village of Aldbury. It was constructed this far away mainly because of the opposition of land owners of the time and not, as is generally believed, because of the Rothschild family who did not arrive in Tring until almost 40 years later! An access road from the town to the station (Station Road) was not built until 1838, several months after the first train had run.

Constructed by more than a thousand navvies, Tring cutting is a tremendous feat of engineering. Millions of tons of earth were excavated entirely by hand to cut a path some 55 feet in depth through the hills for the railway line to run from London to Birmingham. The earth, which was loaded into huge wooden carts, was pulled up along a wooden ramp from the bottom of the cutting to the top by horses guided by one of the navvies. If the rope should break he would have to be very quick to get out of the way before the heavily laden cart ran back onto him and there were many deaths and injuries when this happened. The engineers always preferred to cut through rock rather than dig out soil, because there was less excavating to be done where rock was concerned as the sides of the embankment could be much steeper than with soil. The cutting itself is the highest point on the line. In July 1837 the first train ran to Boxmoor (Hemel Hempstead), and as far as Tring on 16 October. The first journey from Euston to Birmingham took place on 17 November 1837 and took just over four hours.

Tring boasted four cinemas over a 50-year period from 1912-62 but unfortunately only one remains that still looks like having been a cinema—the old Empire Picture Theatre/Gaiety in Akeman Street.

The Gem cinema (1912-16) was sited in the Unity Hall above the Tring Co-operative Society's shop in the lower High Street near the *Robin Hood* public house. Holding some 300 people, it was also used at times for plays, the stage being 19ft. deep. The Gem closed in July 1916 when the new Gem (1916-20) was ready to open. This was a purpose-built cinema in Western Road almost opposite the end of Henry Street and could seat up to 390 people. At the same time that the Gem opened, the Empire (1916-39) in Akeman Street was also opening in direct competition and, as the population of Tring was only some four thousand, competition was fierce. Subsequently the Gem closed in the early 1920s.

The Empire, later in 1932 to be known as the Gaiety, was also purpose-built to hold some 250 people in the stalls and another 64 in a small balcony. The Empire opened a few days before the Gem in Western Road and, on the closing of the Gem in 1920, the Empire/Gaiety became the only cinema in Tring until 1936.

The Regal in Western Road opened on 10 September 1936. During the Second World War it was very popular with servicemen from the American Air Force base at nearby Marworth as well as with evacuated children from London who were billeted in the town. It was purchased by the Mayfair circuit in the early 1940s before all Mayfair cinemas were purchased by A.B.C. (Associated British Cinemas) during

1943. Because of an agreement with cinemas in Aylesbury and Hemel Hempstead, the Regal could not screen any films until three weeks after they had played in these towns. The Regal closed on Saturday 15 February 1958 to a capacity house, and the owners blamed the high rate of entertainment tax as the reason for closing. The author was employed there as a projectionist on this last night, and his uncle, Mr. David Bradding, was the cinema manager. It was re-opened as a cinema for a short period in April 1958 by an independent, and closed again in 1960. It was then rented by the Tring Operatic and Amateur Dramatic Society until it closed for the last time in 1962. The building became derelict and was demolished in 1979.

Tring has seen some considerable changes since the 1980s. There is now the new shopping precinct of Dolphin Square, and at long last the by-pass was constructed through the park, contributing to what is a very pleasant Hertfordshire town.

1 Tring Parish Church and Parsonage Farm from an engraving of *c*.1700. The view would look very different today, as between the church and farm is now Frogmore Street and Dolphin Square. Parsonage Farm was there until the 1950s when the land was eventually used for the building of a new school.

2 An engraving of Tring Parish Church, which is dedicated to St Peter and St Paul, from *c*.1850. It is believed that there has been a church on this site since A.D. 37 as a Roman coin dating from this period was discovered on the line of the old Roman Akeman Street.

3 This photograph was taken in *c.*1905. There are still traces of some original Norman gargoyles in the stonework outside the church. The registers contain entries relating to the ancestors of George Washington who was to become the first President of the United States of America.

4 An aerial view of the town centre. Akeman Street and the crossroads are to the right with Frogmore Street, Dundale, and the allotments running off to the top right. Tring Brewery, the *Rose and Crown*, Bank Alley and Victoria Hall and the old Malthouse are all in the centre area of this 1920 photograph. New Mill is visible in the top right-hand corner.

5 (*above*) In this painting we can clearly see the church and vicarage as well as the old Wren mansion before it was altered, together with Nell Gwyn's Avenue leading down to the road, viewed from Upper Pond Close in the 1700s. The path went to New Mill and was there until the 1970s when houses were built on this land.

6 The church and Parsonage House from a painting of 1829. Extensive renovations took place in the 19th century when two new bells were added. In the church is a monument to Sir William Gore who was Lord Mayor of London (1645) and a founder member of the Bank of England. Also shown is the pond from where the field gets its name.

7 A photograph of the church and vicarage from Upper Pond Close, *c.*1900. Compare this with the painting of 1829 and little, if anything, has changed over the years. The Vestry Hall at the top of Church Lane can be seen to the right.

8 The interior of the church in the 1890s. In 1066 the church would most likely have been made of wood. At some time after the Norman Conquest it was reconstructed of stone. The chantry was added in the early 1300s and at the same time a new chancel floor was laid.

9 Some of Tring's senior citizens in 1875 outside the church to receive Easter Bread which was given each year.

10 The clock mechanism in the church was installed in 1882 at the time of major renovation work. The two dials to the left and right show the time a few seconds before 11 o'clock. The two shafts just to the side of these dials and the one in the centre are for the old hand-winding mechanism.

11 A modern view of the church and War Memorial. The patterned area in front of the memorial depicts the efforts of Walter Rothschild in the successful training of zebras.

12 The vicarage in 1904. A very grand building which dates from the 18th century with extremely decorative barley-stick-curved chimney stacks. The young girl in the doorway is the Reverend Henry Francis's housekeeper. Although the house still remains, it now contains the offices for the Sutton Housing Trust which took over the premises in 1969. The flower beds and lawn have been replaced by an ornamental pond.

13 The archway and gate-house leading through to the vicarage photographed on 6 February 1969. All of this has been preserved; access is gained by the footpath to the rear of the church from Dolphin Square or via Church Yard just off the High Street along the side of the church.

14 Churchyard Cottages next to the vicarage gatehouse, again photographed on 6 February 1969. The cottages have now been renovated and are private dwellings. Through the small archway was a footpath through fields to New Mill village, approximately one mile from Tring. This land has now been built on, the houses reaching all the way to the village.

15 An aerial view of the parish church and the northern side of the High Street taken by the author in 1994. Frogmore Street is to the bottom left, Brook Street and the cattle market are in the top right-hand corner.

16 The first President of the United States of America, George Washington (1732-99), was a direct descendant of the Reverend Lawrence Washington of Tring. One of the reverend's sons, also Lawrence, left Tring for Virginia in 1659, and after returning for a short period he went back to Virginia where he finally settled. At the time of the colonial war, George Washington was Commander in Chief of the American army from 1775 to the end of the struggle in 1783. On the founding of the Republic he became its first President in 1789 serving two terms but refusing election for a third.

17 This engraving after T. Badeslade shows how the park was planned to look at the time of Sir William Gore, c.1700. The carriageway at the bottom right can still be found as can the circle of pine trees. Nell Gwyn's Avenue and the church are in the top left-hand corner. Although the gardens and lakes were never built on this scale, it is possible to walk through the park and identify some of the features.

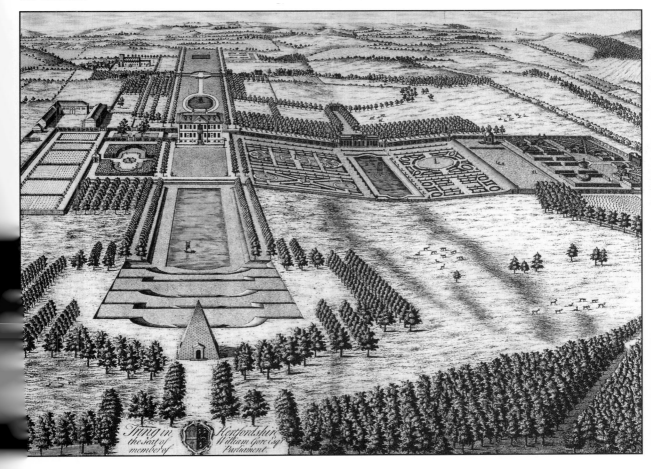

18 Charles II (1630-85) was a frequent guest of Henry Guy at the mansion in the park and entertained Nell Gwyn there. This portrait is by John Michael Wright, or possibly from his studio, and was painted between 1660-65.

19 A line engraving, *c*.1675, of Nell Gwyn by Gerald Valck after Sir Peter Lely. Nell Gwyn was an orange seller and comedy actress from Drury Lane who was a mistress of Charles II and met with him at the mansion. There are many stories about their association, one being that the King gave the mansion to Nell, but this has never been proved.

To the Honourable *Henry Guy of Tring-*
House Esq. this Plate *of y Mannor House is*
Humbly Dedicated *by John Oliver.*

Pa. 593

Oxening's Heats 1700

20 The mansion in 1690 from a print in the *Historical Antiquities of Hertfordshire* by Henry Chaucer. This is how the mansion looked when it was owned by Colonel Henry Guy who commissioned Sir Christopher Wren to design it for him. Henry Guy sold it to Sir William Gore before 1700 and Charles, William's son, sold it in 1768 to Sir Drummond Smith. The estate was sold in 1823 to William Kay. In 1872 it was purchased at auction by Lionel Nathan de Rothschild.

21 This photograph of the mansion before the alterations is from about 1860. Today the mansion bears very little resemblance to this Wren building, and is considered by many people to be of a much inferior design. Today's mansion was virtually built around his original structure.

22 The mansion *c*.1890, showing the reconstruction work being undertaken to the Wren building for the Rothschild family. The wing to the left was added *c*.1874. In this stage of the building the outer façade is almost complete. To prevent the cattle grazing on the lawns there is a ha-ha, fence and hedge, clearly shown in this photograph.

23 Walter Rothschild with his zebra-cart at the mansion, *c*.1900. Walter trained zebras to pull these carts and on one occasion he drove a combination of three zebras and a horse down Piccadilly and into the forecourt of Buckingham Palace. Princess Alexandra attempted to stroke one of the zebras much to the apprehension of Walter! Local blacksmith, Mr. Eric Reed, attended to the zebras' shoes.

24 The south face of the mansion and garden in 1890 shows the stables to the left in the background. The gardens are now landscaped and remain much the same today, except that there are tennis courts where the lawn is to the right.

5 The author's photograph of the fireplace in the smoking room taken in 1994. The interior decorations of pseudo-Greek 'kitsch' marble figures were selected by Nathaniel Rothschild and adorn not only the fireplace, but all the walls which have matching plaques of nude figures, each set in a pink marble surround.

26 The mansion in 1897. The flag is the Royal Standard of the Prince of Wales who was a close friend of Walter Rothschild and was staying at the mansion as a guest of the family. The emus were allowed to roam freely throughout the park in addition to the zebra, wild horses, kangaroos, tortoise and cranes that Walter Rothschild had introduced.

27 Taken in *c*.1910, this photograph shows some of the kangaroos in the park. They were introduced together with many other breeds by Walter Rothschild whose studies and reports about many species of animals and insects were world renowned. This is the south face (rear) of the mansion.

28 This photograph at the turn of the century shows the ha-ha, hedge and fence very clearly. The author was allowed to clear this area of ground in 1994 to expose the wall and remains of the fence. Because of the way a ha-ha is constructed it cannot be seen from the mansion. It is literally a sunken hedge.

29 Coming along the driveway from the High Street presents guests and visitors to the Rothschilds with their first view of the mansion. The photograph was taken in the 1920s. Nell Gwyn's Avenue is to the left of the carriageway.

30 A closer view of the north face (front) entrance, which has remained unchanged since it was re-styled *c*.1890. Some of the rooms on the top floor were used as a nursery and school for the Rothschilds' children. The mansion has been the premises of the Arts Educational School since the 1950s.

31 May Day celebrations with a Children's Festival at the mansion, 1914. The festival was organised by Mrs. Minall, wife of Alfred Minall who was a joiner working on repairs to Walter Rothschild's cottage before becoming one of Walter's taxidermists at the museum.

32 A quiet Sunday afternoon stroll through Tring Park on a summer's day! Although the park was owned by the Rothschilds, parts of it were open to the public. The use of a magnifying glass will reveal more details of the style of dress etc. worn in those days. This photograph was taken the 1920s.

33 Tring Show in the park, *c*.1920. Shows were held each year from *c*.1875, and were greatly supported by the Rothschild family up until Walter Rothschild's death in 1937. Walter would present prizes in the sheep dog competitions. After the Second World War they resumed for a short while until the early 1950s.

34 Nell Gwyn's Avenue, *c*.1930 from the High Street, looking at the north face of the mansion. During the Second World War the Tring 7th Corp of Hertfordshire Battalion Home Guard would parade here together with the Air Raid Precaution wardens and fire brigade. (The author's father was in the 7th Corp of the Home Guard from 1943.)

35 This is the stairway and hall inside the mansion. Walter Rothschild was supposed to have 'bowled' along the marble tiles of the hallway similar to a piano on castors. This photograph was taken in 1890. Apart from the large paintings at the top of the stairs, which have since been removed, it has not altered.

36   London Lodge along the London Road just before the flint and brick wall on the outskirts of the estate as you enter Tring from Berkhamsted. Taken in 1920, this shows another entrance to the park, there being three altogether. There is a summer house on the Oddy Hill just above the lodge. The road was diverted from this point when the Tring by-pass was built.

37   The gates to the park in Park Street, photographed in the 1920s. Unfortunately they were removed in the early 1940s and the metal was used in the war effort. The mechanism for opening and closing the gates was located in the first house. All that remains now are the bases which are still in the roadway.

38 This photograph taken in 1897 looks towards the wall at the end of the gardens in the mansion grounds. All of these houses were built by the Rothschilds during the 1870s and 1880s and are still standing. The small barn, possibly a stable, is no longer there, but the foundations can still be seen.

39 These are the gardens on the other side of the wall in Park Street as they were in 1892. The museum is on the right and the houses on the left are those shown in the previous photograph. The gardens no longer exist and are now overgrown. The author remembers playing here during the late 1940s as well as in the stables which are to the right but not shown.

Louisa Alms Cottages, Park Rd., Tring

40   The Louisa Alms Cottages at the junction of Akeman Street and Park Road in the 1920s. The cottages were so well built that little major repair work has been found necessary over the years. The cottages which were designed by Rothschild's architect William Huckvale were erected in 1893 and extended in 1901.

41   The Museum and Louisa Cottages photographed from Park Road in the 1920s. They were built for Emma Rothschild in memory of her mother and were used by retired employees of the Tring Park Estate. When Walter Rothschild died in 1937, the museum, together with his vast collection of animals, birds, moths and reptiles, was given to the Natural History Museum as an annexe on the understanding that research work should carry on there.

42 The cottage and museum, as seen in 1892 from Park Street. Built for Walter Rothschild as a 21st-birthday present by his mother Emma, Walter intended the museum for his own use. However, in August 1892 (on the same day as the Tring Show in the park) it was opened to the public for the first time, and thereafter attracted some 30,000 visitors annually.

43 The Lily Pond in the park was located near the High Street and is now the site of the Memorial Gardens. The pond had been drained for many years. This photograph was taken at the turn of the century.

44 A view of the mansion from the slope going up into the woods taken in 1892, this scene is just the same today as it was more than 100 years ago.

45 The summer house in the woods above the park in March 1964. In the Rothschilds' time this must have been really magnificent. The area is now almost completely overgrown and all that remains is the front façade which was restored in late 1995.

46 Nell Gwyn's monument in the woods of Tring Park. This photograph from the 1930s is taken from the carriageway leading into the woods from the park. To the left is Wigginton and opposite is the carriageway that leads up to the summer house on the top of the Oddy Hills.

47 The mansion, Walter Rothschild Zoological Museum and Tring Park. Albert Street is in the bottom right-hand corner leading to Akeman Street. The by-pass runs through the park in the top right-hand corner. (Photographed in 1994 by the author.)

48 Part of the Rothschild estate, this is Home Farm in Park Road, *c*.1910. There was a connecting tunnel from the farm to the museum which was used by Walter Rothschild. Upper Icknield Way runs along the skyline where the Goldfield Mills windmill is visible on the left. The open fields below have now been developed into residential areas. Only Goldfield meadow remains today.

49 Home Farm where Walter Rothschild died in 1937. This photograph was taken from Stubbins Wood above the farm. The farm has since been re-named White Cloud Farm and later became the home of the Moss family. Stirling Moss was a world champion racing driver in the 1960s.

50 Outside the *Green Man* in the lower High Street in 1897 we see bunting being put up for the visit to Tring of the Prince of Wales. The prince was a close friend of the Rothschilds and made several visits to them at the mansion. The town was really 'spruced up' as the cut branches on the pavement show.

51 (*left*) Further along the High Street, more bunting and decorations for the visit of the Prince of Wales. Note the poles along the roadside which were especially installed for the occasion with oil lamps strung between them. Electricity came to the mansion and museum in the early 1890s. The old *Rose and Crown* is on the left.

52 (*below*) King Edward VII who, as the Prince of Wales, was a regular guest of the Rothschild family. The similarity between the King and Walter Rothschild is quite remarkable. Walter was very often mistaken for the King when he was seen by Tring inhabitants. It is not known if he was actually addressed as 'your Majesty'!

CUBLINGTON.

NORTHMARSTON.

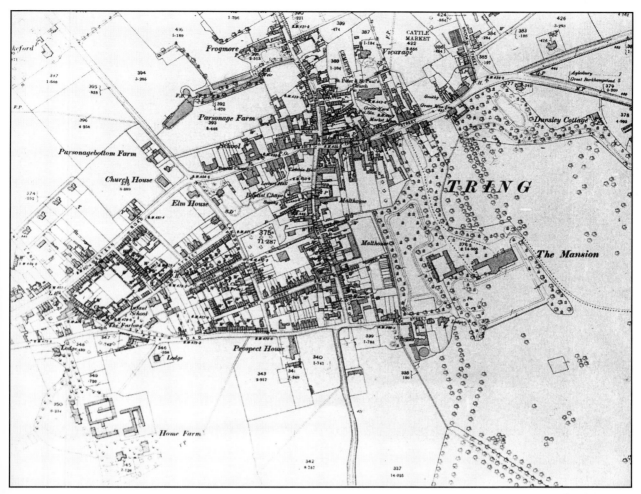

55 (*above*) Tring as it was in 1877. This map shows Nell Gwyn's Avenue running down to the High Street from the mansion. At the bottom is the *Green Man Inn*, also part of the Tring Estate. The double row of trees is still standing today and is best seen from the footbridge crossing the by-pass. The map was produced after the mansion was purchased by the Rothschilds in 1873.

3 (*top left*) Staghounds outside Tring station. Walter Rothschild, who ran a pack of staghounds, had an unfortunate incident with the 'snobs' (nickname of the 600 employees of a local boot factory), when he was dragged from his horse because they took a poor view of the rich enjoying themselves when they, the 'snobs', were suffering hard times. The station master's house is on the right.

4 (*bottom left*) Four photographs of Lord Rothschild's staghounds in villages near Tring. After the incident with the 'snobs', Walter, and the staghounds, never met in Tring again. His father, Nathaniel, was very shaken by the episode. From the top left, the views are of Cubblington, North Marston, Norduck and Creslow.

HENRY VII's
1457-1509

FIREBACK
TRING

CAN YOU READ THE FAMILY TREE?

56 A fireback from somewhere in Tring. The author has reason to believe that it was in fact in the mansion as many of the fireplaces have this type of back to them. This one dates from the time of Henry VII (1485-1509).

57 A common sight at the turn of the century: a German touring band, better known as buskers, playing for pennies, *c*.1900. In the background is the *Kings Arms* on the junction of King Street and Park Road. Over the fence on the right is Old Weavers Place where the weaving shop of Mr. Cato was located.

58 The lower High Street of *c.*1890 looking east. Fulk's hardware shop was an old Tring family business. On the far right is a newspaper office which was demolished by the Rothschilds in 1897 and replaced with a timbered house used by the estate's accountant. The *Plough Hotel* on the left was one of at least seventeen public houses in Tring at the time.

59 The lower High Street, *c.*1880. This photograph shows that there was no entrance to Tring Park and the mansion at this point until sometime just before 1897, the time of the Prince of Wales' visit to the Rothschild family. The entrance was to be located where the ivy-covered building is in the centre of the left-hand row of buildings.

60 The lower High Street, *c.*1890. The white building on the left is the old *Rose and Crown* which was demolished in 1905 when a new building was erected by the Rothschilds. The carriageway and gates to the mansion and park are clearly shown to the left. These were illuminated with electric lights in 1897 when the Prince of Wales visited.

61 The lower High Street in *c.*1890 looking towards the crossroads. Notice the difference in clothes of the period, from the working men's on the right to the well-to-do couple on the left. The shop next to the *Plough Hotel* eventually became John Bly's antique shop when it moved from near the Tring brewery, and the old *Rose and Crown* is visible on the left.

62 The High Street in 1880 looking towards the crossroads. The old *Rose and Crown*, minus its sign, is to the left. The *Bell* public house is next to the far shop with the blinds. It was in an archway by the side of the *Bell* that meat and game was hung from hooks set into the old beams for the *Bell* kitchens. A barber's shop is to the right (see the pole), making two along here, the other being near the Frogmore Street junction.

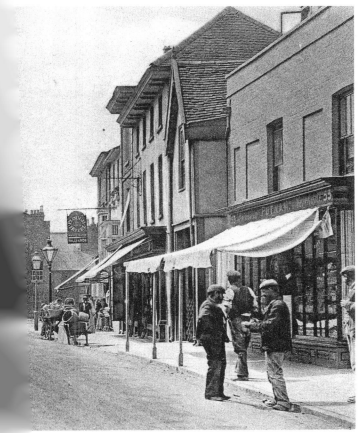

63 The Oddfellows procession outside Butcher's Bank and Bank Alley in the High Street in the early 1880s together with Tring Town Brass Band. The Oddfellows was one of several Friendly Societies that existed in the town. Their annual parade would commence at 3.30 in the afternoon and finish at 5.00 o'clock at the church.

64 This photograph was taken in the 1860s, and shows Butcher's Bank (with railings), Tring Brewery Company entrance (through archway), and John Bly's antique shop (after the white building). Oak Alley or Stink Alley, now known as Bank Alley, is next to the Butcher's Bank.

65 The High Street of 1914. On the left is Westwood and Dellar greengrocer's, followed by Glover's grocery shop, the National and Westminster Bank, Tring Brewery through the archway and then John Bly Antiques. The brewery was owned by John Brown from the 1830s until he sold it to Lock and Smith of Berkhamsted in 1898.

66 A later photograph of the same section of the High Street taken in the early 1950s. Compare the two views and you will see that they are much the same. The major rebuilding of this part of the town did not start until the 1980s. It is a lot different now, as many of the buildings on the right have been demolished. The *Bell Inn* is one of the oldest surviving public houses in Tring.

67 The High Street looking east, *c*.1880. The first building on the left is the Fire Offices. The four shops after this, which are in front of the church, were demolished *c*.1900 The *Plough Inn* is shown in the lower centre of this photograph. The proprietor of the *Rose and Crown* was Mr. J. Sheerman.

68 A view of the High Street in 1880. On the left is the chemist shop of Mr. Bass, known locally as Uncle Bass. The old post office is next at the time a Mr. Clements was the postmaster. The *Bell* is just visible further along the street, and John Bly's shop is on the right.

69 Looking towards the old *Rose and Crown* at the turn of the century we find sheep being driven along the High Street on their way to the cattle market in Brook Street. Greening's outfitters became Raymond Herman's gentlemen's outfitters, but Jack Clement's jewellery shop remained for another 50 years. The *Bell* public house is on the left next to the archway.

70 The crossroads at Frogmore Street, *c*.1880. The man in the bowler hat on the right is a Mr. Knight. The local doctor, Dr. Pope, to Mr. Knight's right, is wearing the silk hat.

71 The old *Rose and Crown* has now been replaced by the new building which is set back from the road. John Bly's antique shop is on the right and Bank Alley is next to it. The large mound at the entrance is an early anti-mugging structure preventing any would-be robber from hiding in the shadows on the corner. Photographed in *c*.1920.

High Street, Tring, looking East.

72 The High Street crossroads showing Akeman Street to the right and Frogmore Street on the left in the late 1890s. This part of the road was called Western Road but was later changed to the High Street in the early 1900s. The second building over the crossroads on the left is the old post office. Note another anti-mugging construction on the lower left where the two men are standing. A barber's shop is on the left with the Tring Brewery, Butcher's Bank (with railings) and the *Rose and Crown* to the right.

73 The crossroads in the late 1930s. Gates' stationery shop on the corner of Frogmore Street, Goddard's newsagents, Mr. Herman's outfitter's shop, Tarmer and Eldridge shoe shop, Rooker's tea room and Clement's jewellers are all along this side before the *Bell*. On the right are Alex Smith's chemist (formerly Jeffery's) and the Chequers café. Mr. Stevens sold music and gramophones.

74 Photographed in *c.*1890, the building on the left is the new Market House built by public subscription when the old building in the High Street was demolished. The lower open area was totally enclosed in 1910. Tring fire brigade later occupied the building. The police station has not yet moved from near the Vestry Hall (which was built in 1866) at the top of Church Lane to a new building to be built next to the Market House.

High Street, Tring

75 Here we have the same view of the High Street (Western Road) from the corner of Frogmore Street in the 1920s. The police station has now been built on the empty ground next to the Market House which is now the town's fire station. The National School is at the top of the hill on the right.

76 Taken in the 1930s, the school is clearly visible on the right at the top of the hill. This is quite an unusual photograph as it was taken at the same time as photograph number 84. The policeman is there, as is the banner advertising luncheons and teas at the *George Hotel*, even the shop blinds are identical. The shops to the right are much the same today, although the Market House is no longer the fire station. It was considerably altered in 1993-94.

77 The new post office in the 1880s. The postmaster at the time was Mr. William Rodwell. Deliveries were four times each weekday at 6.00 am, 9.00 am, 4.00 pm and 6.00 pm. On the right is the National School and Ivy Cottage. Note the absence of shops on this side, which were not to be built until Ivy Cottage was demolished. This shows that this part of Tring was not yet fully developed.

78 A horse and coach being driven through the upper High Street. This photograph was taken after 1876, probably towards 1890. The building to the left at the front of the picture is now Tring Conservative Club, with Grace's hardware shop next to it and then the *George Hotel*. Mr. Jeffery has the chemist shop on the corner of Akeman Street.

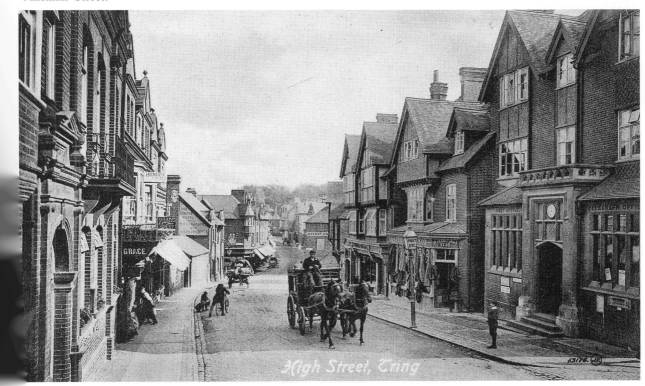

79 Tring's Midsummer Fair. The parade of *c.*1910 led by Tring Band along the High Street. The band would perform at the town's functions and was very popular. During the early 1900s it would play for donations to pay for new uniforms. At one function in the park at Hastoe Lane the band gave a promenade concert and dance, making a nominal charge to raise funds.

80 The High Street of 1890. The ivy-covered building on the left is Ivy Cottage. The wooden building in the centre was later pulled down and the new police station was subsequently built on the ground.

81 This is a better view of the shops on top of the hill along Western Road during the late 1890s. The proprietor of Waldock's tea room, bread and cake shop is standing in his doorway. The shop name still survives above the shop today. The gentleman with the handcart is Joe 'Chops' delivering coal.

82 Another photograph of Western Road, *c*,1910. The delivery van belongs to Mr. Waldock's baker's and confectionery shop.

83 Taken outside the National School, *c.*1910. The *Tring Gazette* Office also sold lace products made by the local cottage industry which thrived in the town. The wall and entrance to the school playground is just shown in the bottom left corner. Note the furniture and linoleum on sale outside Brandon's furniture shop.

84 The opposite view from photograph number 76. The *George Hotel* is owned by the Aylesbury Brewery Company and offers luncheons and teas. Alex Smith now has the chemist shop on the corner of Akeman Street where it became established for many years. Outside the police station the traditional 'blue lamp' is hanging. The gate at the extreme left corner is the entrance to the school.

85 Taken in the 1950s, on the right is Mr. Child's shoe shop, Bagnell watch makers, the post office, Pitkin's dairy shop, Grace's hardware shop. The International Stores and the *George Hotel* are on the left. The lorry belongs to F.W. Metcalfe, another well known local company. The only business remaining today is Grace's shop which now also occupies the old International Stores building.

86 Tring's oldest inhabitant, James Stevens, died on 12 February 1911 aged 103. Born at Astrope near Tring on 16 January 1808, he lived under six monarchs. He was employed as an agricultural labourer at Astrope as well as working on the Tring Park Estate when the Reverend James Williams lived there. The last 15 years of his working life was spent at Home Farm which was occupied by Mr. James Dawe. He retired when he reached the good age of 75, and lived with a daughter in Miswell Lane until his death. He left 52 descendants.

87 Market day in the lower High Street, *c.*1880. The grant was made by Edward II (1284-1327) on 23 July 1315 when a market was allowed on each Tuesday and a fair could be held for 10 days each year.

88 Market day in 1895. The main part of the market was on the other side of the road as in the previous photograph. Today's market is located just opposite here selling a wide range of goods but no livestock. Nell Gwyn's Avenue and the mansion are on the other side of the low wall.

89 Photographed in 1994, this shows the location of the old Gem cinema which was in the Unity Hall on the top floor from 1912-16. The cinema held some 300 people and, as well as films, plays were performed on its 19-foot-wide stage. Access is through the door next to the shop. The Gem closed in July 1916 when the new Gem opened in Western Road.

90 The top of Akeman Street, *c.*1870. The *Royal Oak* (see the sign) and Oak or Bank Alley is on the right. The lady in the crinoline dress is at Evans the Silk Weavers. The building with the thatched roof is Tring Town Farm, now the site of the Walter Rothschild Zoological Museum.

91 Further along Akeman Street, near the top of Park Road. On the left are the *Jolly Sportsman* and *Swan* public houses. The *Jolly Sportsman* was demolished to make way for the Louisa Cottages, although the *Swan* remains as a private house. Note that Tring Town Farm now has a tiled roof instead of the original thatch.

92 Akeman Street, *c.*1870. The shop belongs to Charles Grace, a member of one of Tring's oldest families. The entrance to Albert Street is where the fence is and the cottages on the left were some of the slums that the Rothschilds cleared. The author was born in one of the rebuilt cottages which would have been second along from the archway. The cottage at the very top facing down the street is the Quaker Meeting House.

93 The Quaker Meeting House on the corner of Hastoe Lane and Park Street, *c.*1900. A burial ground to the rear holds the graves of 80 members of the Society of Friends. The meeting house later became a private cottage and was eventually demolished, although the graves are still there today.

94 Outside Grace's maltings and malthouse (on the right) in Akeman Street. To the left is the *Harrow* public house, opposite Mr. Burr's barber's shop. The Victoria Hall and the cross roads with Frogmore Street are in the centre of this 1890s photograph.

95 The malthouse and maltings in Akeman Street in July 1976. These buildings are still there but have now been converted to private accommodation. At the time of the developments in and around Church Lane and the High Street, many fine old buildings were demolished to make way for Dolphin Square, but these have survived.

96 This view of Akeman Street in *c*.1870 shows the Assembly Hall on the left with Mr. Brandon's furniture shop beneath. Both the Assembly Hall and shop were demolished to make way for the Victoria Hall in 1886. The *Harrow* public house is the second building on the right and was pulled down in 1958.

97 These ladies, photographed in 1896, are straw plaiters who lived at Harrow Yard in Akeman Street. Although they have come out to see a funeral go by, they are still busy straw plaiting! Very much a cottage industry, the trade eventually died out due to the import of plait from Italy and the Far East. The *Harrow* public house is on the right. When the council houses in Miswell Lane were built they were moved from here to occupy them.

98 This is the *Harrow* public house in Akeman Street shortly before it was demolished in 1958. Commercial premises now occupy the site. All that remains is the name Harrow Place on the side of an adjoining building.

99 This photograph taken in *c*.1910 shows the Victoria Works in Akeman Street where cider and mineral water were produced. Now called the Victoria Hall, it was erected in 1886 on the site of assembly rooms built in 1825, and was designed by Tring architect William Huckvale. Housing Tring Library for many years, it is now used for meetings and exhibitions.

100 One of the few surviving photographs of the old Empire/Gaiety cinema in Akeman Street taken in 1970. Originally named the Empire in 1916, the name was changed to the Gaiety in 1932. It was purpose-built and could seat 314 people; 250 in the stalls and 64 in a small balcony. This cinema closed during the Second World War and never re-opened.

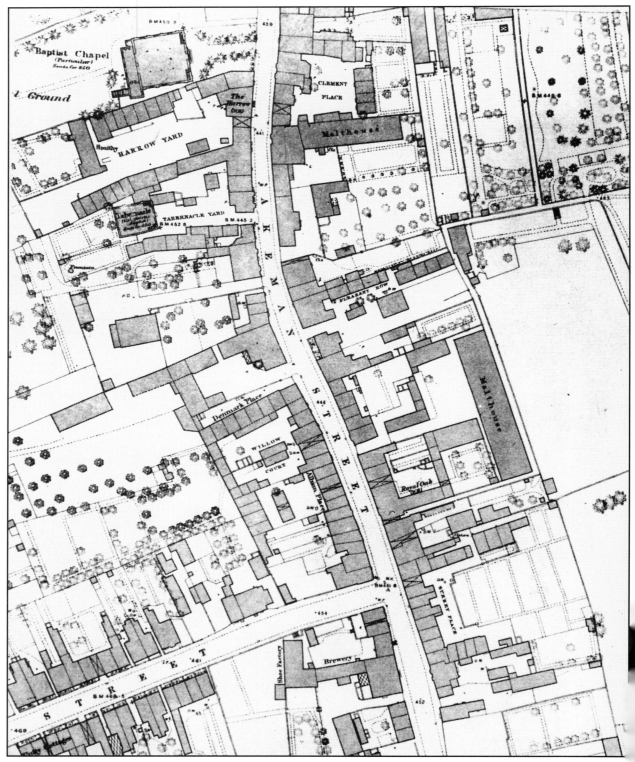

101 Detailed map of the Akeman Street area of 1877. Tring Brewery, the *Harrow* public house, Tring Park Estate land (bottom right), the *Royal Oak* with Bank or Oak Alley alongside it are all shown. Surrey Place, where the author was born, is in the bottom right-hand corner. His cottage is the second one from the archway which is marked with crossed lines.

102 The old Market House in Church Square, *c*.1890. Described as 'an edifice on wooden pillars, having a pillory and cage underneath'. This was the original site before the building was demolished in 1900. Charles II decreed that corn and straw plait were sold in the morning and corn after mid-day. From the 1680s the building was also used as a court. Whipping posts and stocks were frequently used for guilty offenders.

103 Another view of the old Market House with the County Fire Office above Elliman's shop, and the *Plough* public house in the lower High Street, *c*.1890. The shop next to the *Plough* became John Bly's antique shop in later years.

104 Akeman Street and Western Road junction in 1890. The building on the corner was demolished to make way for the new Market House in c.1905. Mr. Mead's butcher's shop and the wooden building were also pulled down to make way for the council offices and new police station.

105 The new Market House on the corner of Akeman Street was built by public subscription at a cost of £2,400. It was erected to replace the old Market House and also to commemorate the Queen's Diamond Jubilee. William Huckvale was the architect.

106 The cavalry outside the Market House on manoeuvres shortly before the First World War. The buildings in the background were stables which were used by the soldiers for their horses. Walter Rothschild was a Major in the Bucks Imperial Yeomanry in 1903.

107 Tring Brass Band on parade outside the mansion, *c.*1870. This photograph was possibly taken a short time after the Rothschild family purchased the mansion and estate in 1873. The band gained popular appeal throughout the 1870s and into the 1920s. In 1903 new uniforms were purchased and a press report states that they 'were very smart in appearance'. These tunics look very similar to those worn by the Salvation Army band from the Citadel in Albert Street.

108 Park Road looking towards Walter Rothschild's museum at the junction of Akeman Street and Hastoe Lane, *c.*1895. The houses remain much the same today as they are in the photograph. The path to the right leads up to Prospect House School which was next to Home Farm.

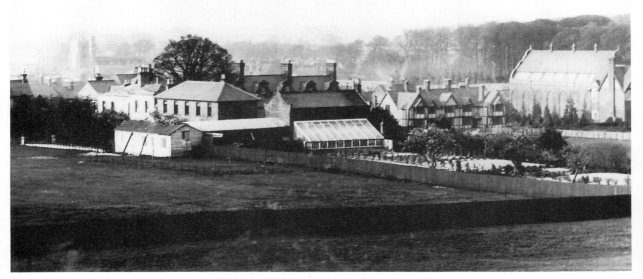

109 Prospect House School from the Downs in 1897. From right to left are the museum and Louisa Cottages on the corner of Akeman Street. The small wooden building is the school's gymnasium. The church is to the far left, while to the right, where the trees are, is part of the Park Estate and the mansion.

110 Looking across Tring from the top of the Downs, *c.*1910. Prospect House and the school have now been demolished. (They would have been in the field to the left.) Langdon Street and the *Castle* public house are to the lower left, while the church and Methodist Chapel (triangular roof to the left) are clearly visible. Mr. Cato's weaving shop was located in Langdon Street until it moved to Charles Street.

111 Mr. Cato's weaving shop in the early 1900s. While weaving was not one of the major industries of the town, it did give employment to many people over a 30-year period.

112 The interior of the weaving shop in 1905. The bearded man standing to the right is Mr. Cato and a Mr. Ward is seated. Schoolboys were employed in the shop and were known as 'half timers'. The business eventually moved to Charles Street until it closed in 1920.

113 With the arrival of the railway it was necessary to provide transport to and from the station which was some two miles from the town. In this photograph, taken in Park Road, we see the station omnibus outside Victoria Cottages on its route through Tring.

114 Ivy Cottage, the School House and National School from the bottom of Western Road (High Street). The National School was founded in *c.*1842 teaching approximately 100 boys and 70 girls in two separate buildings. It expanded in the 1860s to accommodate more children. In the First World War (1914-18) it was used as a Military Hospital. The school house, which was occupied by the Headmaster, together with the school was demolished in the 1980s. All that now remains is part of the wall facing the road. The site is now used by Tring Library and a car park.

115 Ivy Cottage in the early 1800s, next to it is the carpenter's shop for Pendley Manor. The cottage was used by Miss Wilson to teach children the art of straw plaiting. It was demolished to make way for shops at the end of the 1890s. The National School is at the rear.

116 The church and manse on top of the High Street in the early 1920s. The house and church still exist, although more houses have been built next to the manse. Western Road starts just past the flint and brick wall; prior to the early 1900s it began from the Akeman Street crossroads.

117 The top of the High Street and Western Road in the early 1900s. To the left are three businesses in one building: a newsagent and tobacconist's on the ground floor, a printer and bookbinder upstairs, and to the rear through a side entrance was the hairdresser's. Dennis' the saddler's is the shop with the blinds and is still there. The church and manse are to the right.

118 Western Road from the junction with Christchurch Road in 1914 looking towards the *Britannia* public house. To the right is Christchurch Road, at the bottom of it was Parsonage Bottom Farm. Most of the land on this side up to Miswell Lane and Goldfield Meadow was grazed by cattle from the farm which was demolished and whose land was developed in the early 1950s for council housing. This part of the town was always quieter due to the absence of many shops.

119 The Regal cinema in Western Road during 1946. Opening in 1932, it was purchased from the Mayfair circuit by Associated British Cinemas in the early 1940s. The building was demolished in 1979 and the site now contains flats called Regal Court.

120 Western Road from the corner of Miswell Lane, *c*.1910. The *Anchor* public house on the right was a cottage before it was opened as a public house in 1870, when the landlord was George Barber.

121 Taken in October 1906, this is the Tring Co-operative Industrial and Provident Society store on the corner of Charles Street and Langdon Street. The shop was there until the 1960s when it was closed. It is now a private house.

122 The old *Rose and Crown*, *c*.1900. There has been a *Rose and Crown* on this site since *c*.1620. The excise offices were located here from the 17th to the middle of the 19th centuries. With the coming of the railway in 1837 the London and North Western Railway Company had their booking office here. The gate to the park is just visible past the cart.

123 A better view of the old *Rose and Crown*, photographed in *c*.1900. The building was demolished *c*.1905 and replaced with a building designed by William Huckvale for the Rothschild family. Through the arch was a bowling green and the grounds were large enough for fairs to be held there.

124 Tring's best known inn is the new *Rose and Crown*. This is a view from the church tower taken during the late 1940s; the park and Tring Downs are in the background. Built mainly for guests of the Rothschild family, it had several royal visitors including the Prince of Wales, whose signature is in the guest book.

125 The *Green Man Inn* which was part of the Tring Park Estate. In this photograph of *c*.1900 the publican, Mr. Woodman (with the long bushy beard), is standing in the doorway. The brewery next to the *Green Man* is probably that of John Philby who brewed at the *Green Man* from 1846. Even the postman managed to get into the photograph!

126 The original *George* public house on the corner of Frogmore Street, *c*.1890. It was extended in *c*.1897 by the Aylesbury Brewery Company when the adjoining building was demolished to make way for it. In 1806 it was described as a 'small hotel and corn chandlers' and was owned by a Joseph Tompkins. The *George* finally closed in the late 1980s.

127 Brook End, now known as Brook Street, *c*.1870. To the left is the Malt House. The building on the right is Wigginton Manor owned by Mr. Edwin Smith; the road in front of the house leads up to Mortimer Hill. The cattle market would eventually be located where the last row of cottages is standing.

128 The *Robin Hood* public house on the corner of Brook Street, *c.*1890. It was at this time owned by Roberts and Wilson Brewery of Ivinghoe. Next to it is William Bly's antique shop (no relation of John Bly). The house to the right on the corner of Mortimer Hill no longer stands. Tring cattle market is just past the cottages on the left.

129 Another view of Brook Street. This is from the corner of Station Road, taken about 1912, and shows the *Robin Hood* public house which dates from the 17th century. William Bly's antique shop, a row of cottages and the cattle market are at the far right and all of these buildings remain today, although the junction has changed dramatically over the years.

130 The *Britannia* public house *c.*1910, originally built by John Brown of the Tring Brewery in *c.*1830 for the navvies working on the London to Birmingham railway. The blocks in front were some of the original sleepers used on the railway. In this photograph it is owned by Lock and Smith Breweries of Berkhamsted which purchased Tring Brewery in 1898. The land on the right is now occupied by the Woodland Close housing estate which was built in 1948, the first council estate in Tring.

131 With the *Britannia* public house in the distance, this photograph shows the *Bricklayers Arms* on the corner of Duckmore Lane, *c.*1870. The *Bricklayers Arms* was demolished at the turn of the century and the ground now forms part of the allotments which are still used today. Next to the yew trees to the right is a row of cottages which was known as Bottle Cross. Mr. Hobbs' stone masons' yard was also here.

132 Two views of the *Harrow* public house in Akeman Street a few weeks before it was demolished in 1958. A fine old building and part of old Tring, it was a sad loss when it was finally pulled down. Akeman Street is one of the older parts of Tring and lost a number of old buildings during the late 1950s and 1960s.

133 In this view of the *Harrow* we are looking along Akeman Street with the Victoria Hall to our rear. In 1890 the publican was Miss Ann Miller. Past the archway was Warrior's baker's shop. The Methodist Chapel gates are on the right.

134 Miswell Lane, also called Windmill Lane, in 1910. To the right is Goldfield Meadow before several rows of houses were built adjacent to the road. Osmington Boys' School was built between these houses and Christchurch Road. At the top of the road is a windmill which still stands although without its sails.

135 Miswell Lane looking towards the Downs in 1915. The name Miswell, or 'Musse-well', is derived from a spring and water course which rose by Miswell Farm and flowed to Tring Ford, where it converged at Little Tring with the water course from Dundale.

Goldfield Mills Tring

Photo C. A. Howlett

136 Goldfield Mills windmill at the top of Miswell Lane and the junction of Icknield Way. Built in 1840 by Mr. Groves who was a partner with the Mead family of the Mead Flour Mill in New Mill. After a disagreement with the family he built the mill to continue in business on his own. The main structure still remains and has now been converted into private accommodation. This photograph was taken during the early 1900s.

137 Upper Icknield Way and the Goldfield Mills windmill in *c*.1905. The Upper Icknield Way starts in Ivinghoe village and passes the outskirts of Tring on its way to Wendover. Part of the old Roman way, it is named after the ancient British Iceni tribe.

138 Champneys, on the outskirts of Tring, was purchased by Nathaniel Rothschild for his wife Emma, for use as a possible dower house in the event of her ever deciding to leave the mansion in Tring Park to make way for the younger family. Following the death of her youngest son Charles in 1923, she decided to sell Champneys. Today, it is a college for health and beauty.

139 Tring fire brigade. The fire engine was horse-drawn and was in service for almost 200 years! This photograph was probably taken during one of the Tring Shows in the park when the brigade would be called upon to demonstrate their fire-fighting capabilities. The firemen were all volunteers.

140 The fire brigade outside their station in the Vestry Hall at the top of Church Lane. Many of the firemen in this photograph were employed by local shop-owner Gilbert Grace. The fireman standing fourth from the right is John Bly, grandfather of the John Bly of television antiques fame.

141 This photograph, taken on 12 October 1927, is of the official reception for the new Baico-Tonner motor fire engine for the Tring Fire Brigade which replaced the out-dated horse-drawn fire engine. Front row, left to right: Councillor W.N. Mead, Councillor T.N. Hedges, Councillor John Bagnall, Councillor John Bly, Councillor A.J. Tompkins, Mr. H.J. Gurney (Finance Officer to the Council), Councillor H.J. Baldock, and Councillor G. Goddard. Second row: Caretaker F.J. Reeve, Firemen E. Brittain, F. Rance, W. Cooper, and J. Copcutt, Chief Officer G. Putnam, Driver W. Keele and Third Officer A. Hedges. Third row: Firemen A. Underwood and W. Welling.

142 Sunday school outing possibly from the Salvation Army in Albert Street of *c*.1920. These outings were probably the only occasions on which many people were able to get away for a day out and were a social event not to be missed. Most trips would be to the nearby countryside, or along the canal by barge.

143 Frogmore Street in 1890. Most of the buildings on the right have now disappeared. On the left is the manse for New Mill Chapel, followed by what was to become Johnson's wet fish shop in the 1940s. The entrance to Church Lane is just before the *Dolphin* public house, a second, as yet unknown, public house or brewery is further down, while in the distance is Barnet's Bakery.

144 A photograph of Alma Place, also known as Big Place, just off Frogmore Street, *c.*1900. Westwood Lane is to the right and Barnet's Bakery is off to the left of this. The business still exists today although Alma Place was demolished in the early 1900s.

145 This photograph shows the cottages in Church Lane opposite the Vestry Hall. Taken during the early 1930s, it shows Mrs. Prior standing outside her home. None of these old cottages exists now; they were demolished to make way for the Dolphin Square shopping precinct named after the *Dolphin* public house which once stood here.

146 A better view of the same cottages, again taken during the 1930s. Looking towards Frogmore Street, the *Dolphin* public house was at the bottom on the right. This was also one of the last remaining cobbled paths in Tring.

Church Lane, Tring

147 Parsonage Place off Frogmore Street, *c*.1920. The building at the end of the cottages was to become Johnson's wet fish shop which was there for many years from the late 1930s. Photograph number 143 shows this better, although it was not a shop then.

148 Back-breaking work—reaping corn by hand. An un-named farmer during the 1880s. After the corn was reaped it had to be bundled into sheafs and stacked, also by hand.

149 Harvesting the corn, *c.*1900. Mr. Sear is seen here with the Pratt family near Holly Mead Farm on the outskirts of Tring. A very hard occupation in those days, as most of the work was manual, although mechanisation was in use as the straw bales to the left show.

150 The construction of Tring Cutting, from an oil painting of 1837. Built for the London and North Western Railway Company, it clearly shows the navvies and the methods used to remove earth up the sides to waiting horse and carts at the top. One of the most dangerous tasks was guiding the barrows of earth along the wooden ramps. If the rope should break, as often happened, the navvies had to jump clear before the heavy barrow rolled back on them.

151 This fatal accident happened on Monday 1 June 1908 at Tring railway station sidings. Several coal trucks were being shunted along a siding, the points of which were incorrectly set, when these trucks ran into others that were in the yard. The force of the collision drove some trucks on top of those in the yard, trapping John Higby between the buffers killing him instantly. He worked at the yards loading coal from the trucks into sacks. He was 17 years old and lived at the Harrow Yard in Akeman Street. Another lad named Butler, who was working with him, was seriously injured.

152 The railway station at Tring. Constructed some two miles out of the town mainly because of objections from local land-owners, it was built as part of the London to Birmingham rail link (London and North Western Railway). This photograph shows it in 1905. The woods in the distance are part of Ashridge.

153 The construction of Tring Cutting was a remarkable feat of engineering. Hundreds of navvies cleared millions of tons of earth by hand to enable the railway line to be laid in the 1830s. The cutting is at the same level as the dome of St Paul's Cathedral. This line was part of the London and North Western Railway.

154 This photograph was taken in the early 1920s near Bulbourne on the Tring Summit. It is the highest navigable waterway in England with a fall of 400 feet along two-and-a-quarter miles, having a total of 57 locks.

155 The canal at Marsh Croft Bridge, *c.*1910. Opened in 1805, the canal system was used to transport goods from London and Birmingham. This photograph shows two empty barges being pulled by a horse along the tow path.

View from Canal Bridge, Marsh Croft, Tring.

Photo
C.A.Howlett
Tring

156 An Akeman Street outing in 1897. With New Mill in the background, these happy young ladies and gentlemen are enjoying a boat ride along the Wendover Arm of the Grand Junction Canal, approaching Little Tring pumping station.

157 The Grand Union Canal just along from the flour mill in New Mill is part of the Aylesbury Arm. It was used extensively in the 1800s for the carriage of corn, flour and building materials. This part of the canal used to run as far as Wendover, but it was closed at Little Tring and the canal was drained. This was photographed at the turn of the century.

158 The flour mill on the Grand Union Canal at New Mill Wharf. Boats were constructed here and on this site stood a windmill belonging to the Mead Flour Mills Company until 1911. The field to the right is Gamnel and now contains houses.

159 The Grand Union Canal from the top of the bridge as you leave New Mill going down to the reservoirs. In the distance are Pitstone and Ivinghoe with the cement works' chimneys on the horizon. Until the 1960s there was an abandoned small-gauge rail track running along this stretch. The photograph was taken in the early 1900s.

160 About one mile from Tring lies the village of New Mill. This photograph was taken from outside the allotments near the junction of Icknield Way and Bulbourne Road at the turn of the century. The building in the centre is the *Pheasant Inn* public house now re-named the *New Mill*. The large granite stones in the retaining wall outside the entrance were some of the original sleepers used on the London to Birmingham railway.

161 The Implement Gate which was for many years in New Mill. This gate is well known and shows farming tools from the 19th century. The gate has now been moved from this site to Marsworth village.

162 The Feeder in Brook Street which runs from Tring through New Mill and on to Tringford. Taken in 1913, this photograph shows the gas works in the background. This land was cleared to build houses for the Rothschilds but the project was abandoned when it was discovered that the ground was too waterlogged. To the right is a footpath which went from New Mill through Upper Pond Close to the rear of the church.

163 The Hollow Way at the top of Upper Icknield Way leading down to Drayton Beauchamp, a village on the outskirts of Tring. This was taken *c.*1910.

164 A view of Tring from the Downs. This was taken in 1915 and shows Park Road with the *Castle* public house, the Louisa Alms Cottages, museum, parish church and the Methodist Chapel. Tring by-pass runs through here now, but the trees in the fields are still there today as are the fences. The Prospect House and School were to the left.

165 This view of Tring is from Stubbins Wood and shows Park Road, the church, the Methodist Chapel in Akeman Street (see the large pointed roof between the trees), the museum and mansion to the far right. To one walking through the woods today, this panorama has changed little. The photograph was taken in 1904.

166 Stubbins Wood is to the south of Tring behind Home Farm and Woodland Close. This photograph was taken at the turn of the century and shows one of the many leafy footpaths that run through the wood to West Leith and Hastoe.

167 Taking the road from the junction of Akeman Street and Park Road into Hastoe Lane will bring you to this road which is approximately one mile out of Tring. To the left is Tring Park Estate and the road on the left will take you to Chesham up Marlin Hill, whilst the other goes up Hastoe Hill and past Evans Springs, *c.*1910.

168 The junction in Duckmore Lane. The left-hand road leads to West Leith and the Stubbins Wood to the south of Tring. At West Leith was Mr. Pitkin's dairy farm. Mr. Pitkin also had a farm shop near the police station where he sold the produce from his farm, mainly eggs, cheese, cream and, of course, milk. The shop is now a bank.

169 The cattle market in Brook Street near the *Robin Hood* public house. There has been a market here since the mid-1880s. The building in the centre is the office of Brown and Merry auctioneers and is still there today as are most of the original cattle and sheep pens. The house to the left was eventually demolished and the Market Garage owned by Mr. Andrews was built on the site. This photograph was taken *c.*1900.

170 A later photograph of the cattle market, *c.*1920. Although this photograph shows only sheep, cattle and pigs were also auctioned here each week. Before the introduction of cattle lorries, herds of cows and sheep were driven along the roads to the market before and after the sales.

171 Hard to recognise now, but this is Lower Dunsley, *c.*1870, looking towards Berkhamsted from the *Robin Hood.* One of Tring's many breweries, the Manor Brewery, is on the right and may have been part of the Tring Park Estate. Mr. Burgess' weaving shop is next to the brewery.

172 The junction of Brook Street and the lower High Street, *c.*1900. The *Robin Hood* on the corner is much the same today. The Unity Hall, site of the old Gem cinema, is through the white-arched doorway next to the Co-operative Society's shop, along the hill with the horse and cart outside.

173 From Pond Meadow showing Lower Dunsley. The church is to the right, with the *Robin Hood* (left of white building), and the *Green Man* public house is to the left on top of the rise. There was at one time a very small pond here next to the main road out of the town. Although now completely dry, its shape can still be seen. In later years the meadow was used by the many travelling fairs that toured the country in the summer months. Photographed in 1880.

174 The Great Strike of 1921. A welcome cup of tea or coffee for lorry drivers during the General Strike. Because supplies of coal were disrupted, the Tring Gas, Light and Coke Company gave notice that supplies of gas would be disconnected from 10.30 in the evening to 6.30 the following morning. If no coal 'was forthcoming then the entire gas supply may be suspended'. Appeals were made by the Automobile Association and Motor Union for owners of cars and motor cycles, with drivers, to be put at their disposal.

175 24 July 1939 and Tring is subjected to a shower of hailstones of record proportions as this photograph shows. Not a very good start to the fête and carnival week which was being held at the time!

HAILSTORM
AT TRING
JULY, 24. 1939

176 A typical postcard of 1905, sold as a souvenir of Tring. There is no doubt that Tring was a very popular town to visit for holidays during the late 1800s and early 1900s. Five views are on this particular example, the Implement Gate in New Mill, the museum, the church, New Mill and the High Street.

177 Aldbury village is approximately three miles from Tring and is well known for the original stocks by the village pond, shown in this photograph from 1905. The elm tree, which was about 200 years old, is just visible to the right. It is no longer there, being felled in 1976 when it became unsafe. A simple plaque now marks the place where it once stood.

178 Pendley Mansion in Station Road on the outskirts of Tring. After the Battle of Hastings (1066) the manor of Pendley was given to Robert of Mortain by William the Conqueror, as was Upper Dunsley. It was abandoned in the 19th century by Sir William Harcourt who objected to the building of the railway. It was burned down in 1835 and rebuilt later by Joseph Williams.

179 Overlooking Tring Park and No-Mans Friend Wood from Pendley Beeches on the A41 towards Northchurch in the 1900s. These lovely beech trees were pulled down in the 1960s when the road was widened and improved. The old Roman road of Akeman Street ran through here.

180 Ashridge Monument is situated in the woods just above Aldbury village. It was built to commemorate the founder of inland navigation, Lord Bridgewater, who died in 1803. It was while workmen were building a new access road here in 1870 that they unearthed a hoard of British and Roman coins. This photograph was taken in 1904.

181 Tring town centre in 1994, photographed by the author. Akeman Street crossroads are in the bottom right corner, the High Street is running vertically, with Station Road and Brook Street leading off at the roundabout. The parish church, *Rose and Crown*, Victoria Hall, Dolphin Square and cattle market are all easily seen, as are many of the other buildings and streets already illustrated in previous photographs.

Bibliography

Branch Johnson, W., *Hertfordshire Inns, Part Two* (1963)
Eyles, Allen, and Skone, Keith, *The Cinemas of Hertfordshire* (1985)
Richards, Sheila, *The History of Tring* (1974)
Rothschild, Miriam, *Dear Lord Rothschild, Birds, Butterflies and History* (1983)
Various un-named contributors, *The Peasants Revolt in Hertfordshire 1381* (1981)
Watkins, Clifford L., *The History of Tring School* (1993)

Index

Roman numerals refer to pages in the Introduction, and arabic numerals to individual illustrations.

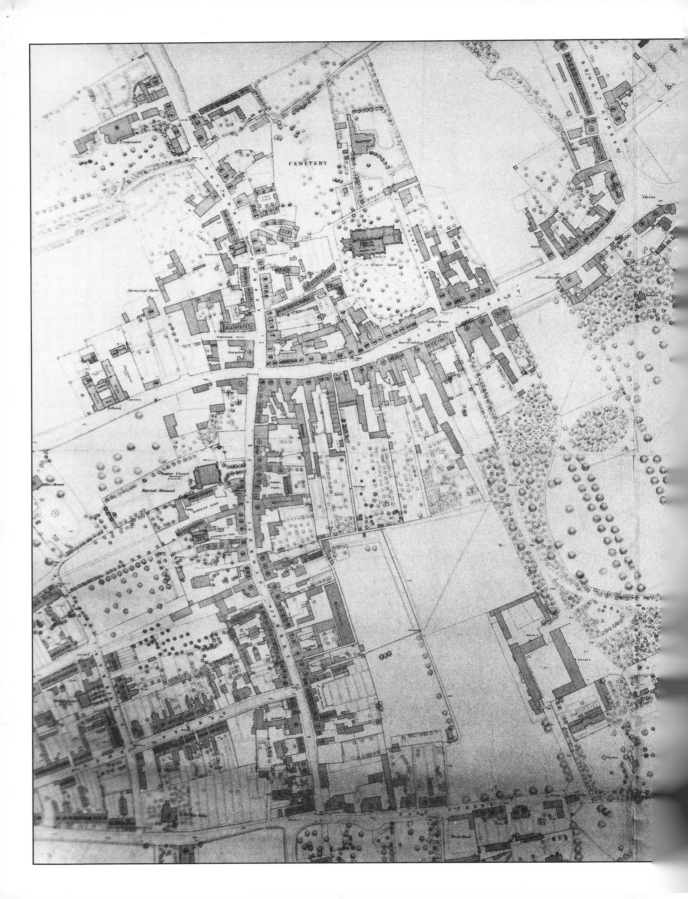